THE STONE AGE

A History from Beginning to End

D1714347

Table of Contents

Introduction

In the early years of the nineteenth century, an antiquarian named Christian J. Thomsen was appointed to oversee the cataloging and display of ancient artifacts in the city of Copenhagen in Denmark. In his attempts to develop a coherent way of identifying the periods from which these items came, Thomsen developed a system of classifying ancient civilizations that is still in use today. What came to be known as the three-age system provided a chronology for prehistory (the period of human history before written records) based on technological development. Thomsen called the three periods the Stone Age, when most artifacts were made from stone and flint, the Bronze Age, when the first metal artifacts were created, and the Iron Age, from which time more advanced examples of metalworking were found.

These periods aren't completely separate, and there are considerable overlaps as bronze and ironworking developed in different areas at different times, but broadly, the Bronze Age began around 3,000 BCE and continued until around 1,200 BCE. The Iron Age began in 1,200 BCE, but agreeing when it ended was problematic. Thomsen's view was that the Iron Age marked the end of prehistory and ended with the first development of writing, even though in some areas (Mesopotamia, for example), the development of writing actually preceded ironworking. Nevertheless, Thomsen's notion of dividing the prehistory of human society into three ages was widely adopted and is still, in modified form, used today.

The Stone Age was different, mainly because it covered an enormous span of time, from the emergence of the first human species around 2.6 million years ago up to the beginning of the Bronze Age. Subsequently, this age was further subdivided into three eras: Paleolithic, Mesolithic, and Neolithic. The word *lithic* is Latin and means "stone" while *paleo, meso,* and *neo* mean, respectively, "old," "middle," and "new." While there are disputes about the precise periods to which these terms apply, Paleolithic is generally used to denote a period from around 2.6 million years ago to around 10,000 BCE. Mesolithic means the period from 10,000 BCE to around 5,000 BCE. Neolithic indicates the period from 5,000 BCE to around 3,000 BCE.

These are vast spans of time; the Paleolithic Era alone represents over 99% of the entire history of human development! Yet even today, we know relatively little about the Stone Age world, and our deductions and estimates are based entirely on the interpretation of a relatively small number of artifacts. Most of what we think we know about the longest (and arguably the most important) span of human history is based on little more than educated guesses.

Chapter One

What was the Stone Age?

"The transition to agriculture in the Neolithic was arguably one of the most drastic lifestyle changes in human history."

—Katherine J. Latham

The oldest era of the Stone Age, today called the Paleolithic period, was also the longest. It dates from the earliest period from which stone artifacts have been found, around 2.6 million years ago, to the end of the most recent Ice Age, around 10,000 BCE. At the beginning of this period, the first species that was identified as part of the genus *Homo* (meaning "human") was *Homo habilis*, itself probably related to an earlier ape-like creature called *Australopithecus africanus*.

We know very little about this early proto-human as only a few fragmentary fossilized remains have been discovered in East and South Africa. This species was first described in the 1960s, and some anthropologists aren't certain that it really is a direct antecedent of modern *Homo sapiens*. *Homo habilis* didn't look a great deal like modern humans; it had a notably smaller brain, and it may also have had more ape-like proportions, with arms and legs of a similar length. Nevertheless, *Homo habilis* may have fashioned and used primitive stone tools by striking a cobble against a larger stone to produce sharp-edged shards that could be used for cutting, which is why the Stone Age is generally thought to have begun with the emergence of this species.

Around two million years ago, another new human species emerged in Africa, known as *Homo ergaster*. These were the first early humans to have what we think of as human proportions, with arms significantly shorter than legs. They were also much taller than many other early humans, with the few examples of which fossilized remains have been found standing around 6 feet (180 centimeters).

Homo ergaster seems to have improved upon the tool-making skills first used by *Homo habilis* by refining flakes chipped off large cobbles to make sharper and more specialized stone tools, probably used to butcher and skin animals. It was also the first human species to move outside Africa, with examples identified in Europe and Asia. The examples from Asia are generally identified as *Homo erectus*, though many anthropologists believe that these are simply examples of *Homo ergaster* that migrated to Asia.

Somewhere around 200,000 to 300,000 years ago, the human species developed as three separate but related groups. These were *Homo sapiens*, principally originating in Africa, *Homo neanderthalensis*, mainly in Europe, and *Homo denisova* in Asia, though in parts of Asia, there appear to have also been relict populations of *Homo erectus* in some isolated areas. Toward the end of the Paleolithic era, around 10,000 years ago, *Homo sapiens* had become the dominant human species. Neanderthals became extinct somewhere around 40,000 years ago, and a lack of remains means that we aren't sure what happened to the Denisovans, though archeology suggests that the last of this species as well as the last groups of *Homo erectus* had become extinct around 20,000 years ago.

The gradual emergence of *Homo sapiens* as the dominant human species is something that we cannot readily explain. For tens of thousands of years, the three human species—*Homo sapiens*, Neanderthals, and Denisovans—co-existed and, in some cases, seem to have interbred. No one has discovered any evidence that supports the notion of a war or a period of conquest between the human species, but by the beginning of the Mesolithic era, *Homo sapiens* was the only remaining human species, and it was this, our species, that would transform Stone Age society, culture, and technology in the Mesolithic and Neolithic periods. Most accounts assume that this was because *Homo sapiens* appeared to have superior cognitive abilities compared to the other human species, as evidenced by the discovery of more sophisticated tool-making techniques and even what appear to be the beginnings of art and religion (though Neanderthal artifacts also show evidence of similar improvements).

All we can really be certain about is that at around the time that the Last Ice Age was finally beginning to recede, Neanderthals, Denisovans, and even the last isolated populations of *Homo erectus* in Asia had vanished completely and forever. The remainder of the Stone Age would belong solely to *Homo sapiens*.

Chapter Two

The First Mesolithic Societies

"The Stone Age didn't end because we ran out of stones."

—Ahmed Zaki Yamani

The first human societies that were more than small family groups seem to have emerged among *Homo sapiens* toward the end of the Paleolithic era and the beginning of the Mesolithic era. These were directly linked to climate change brought about by the end of the most recent Ice Age that saw large parts of the world warming as the ice caps melted and other areas being submerged as sea levels rose. This happened in different areas at different times, which makes it difficult to date precisely.

Because Europe has been the focus of archeology for longer than most other areas, we know more about what happened there and in more detail than most regions. However, it seems probable that development in other places was similar. In Europe, the warming of the climate seems to have affected areas such as the Balkans perhaps as much as 15,000 years ago, but in more northern regions, the effect was less pronounced until perhaps 11,000 years ago. As mentioned before, the spread and expansion of human societies were directly linked to this climate change.

As it became warmer, Europe was covered in forest that gradually replaced the barren steppes left behind when the glaciers initially retreated. Pine, birch, and willow grew to create vast, sprawling forests that covered most of the continent, including present-day Britain (Britain was a peninsula at the beginning of the Mesolithic era, connected to present-day France by a land bridge in what is now the English Channel and to present-day Germany, the Netherlands, and Denmark by a landmass called Doggerland). It was only around 6,500 BCE that Britain became an island separated from continental Europe.

The vast forests that came to cover most of Europe were the home to a whole range of animals, including red and roe deer, auroch (a now-extinct species thought to be the ancestor of modern domesticated cattle), elk, as well as wild sheep and goats. These animals provided a rich source of food for *Homo sapiens,* and in the early Mesolithic era, the first large groups of hunter-gatherers seem to have come together, having discovered that hunting was something most efficiently carried out with large numbers of hunters. These people also gathered and ate berries and nuts that they found in the forests, and most were nomadic, following the game they hunted as the seasons changed. Those living close to the sea used fishing and the gathering of shellfish to acquire food.

Most of what we know of this period comes from archeological findings, and unsurprisingly, stone artifacts have survived much better than items made from organic materials. It seems certain that these people would have used wood as well as stone, but there simply aren't surviving artifacts to tell us about this. We do know that the creation of tools became more advanced, with people using microliths—tiny and very sharp shards of flint or other material that were used as blades for cutting or chopping. These were mounted in handles probably made from wood or from materials such as antlers. Microliths were used to make axes, awls, scrapers, spears, harpoons, arrows, and even tiny fishing hooks. The first nets were also developed in this period to catch fish and small game, and some evidence suggests that *Homo sapiens* also began building the first fish traps in rivers. The development of these new aids to hunting and the gathering of larger groups made the acquisition of food much easier than it had been in the past.

There is also evidence that, during the Mesolithic era, *Homo sapiens* began for the first time to use clay to make vessels used to hold liquids and for storage. In the earliest examples, the clay was probably baked on an open fire to harden it, but somewhere around 8,000 BCE, people in the Near East began to build ovens that were used to parch cereal grains and to make bread. The control of fire in ovens also quickly led to the creation of kilns in which clay items were baked to produce more durable pottery items. The movement of populations and the intermarriage between different groups meant that new ideas spread rapidly across Eurasia.

People who lived close to the sea probably lived in more permanent settlements, while inland dwellers are thought to have been migratory, moving as required to follow the large game animals they hunted. The homes that these people lived in were either circular or rectangular and built using wooden post walls over a sunken base, usually with a hearth in the center. Some findings suggest that there was some form of trade between different groups, with raw materials and finished tools and goods being exchanged. Genetic analysis of artifacts also indicates that there was widespread population movement and interbreeding all across Eurasia.

There have been a number of findings that help us to understand what life was like in the Mesolithic period, but one of the most famous and most studied was a discovery made in 1903 of a Mesolithic skeleton in Britain that became known as "Cheddar Man." Gough's Cave is a massive cave in the Cheddar Gorge located in the Mendip Hills of Somerset, England. It became a popular tourist attraction in the nineteenth century, and in 1903, work to improve drainage of the cave uncovered a skeleton that was initially thought to date from up to 80,000 years ago and was widely reported as being "the earliest Englishman."

The skeleton was of a man who died in his 20s and was around 5 feet 5 inches tall (166 centimeters). It was only much later, as new technology emerged, that we began to learn more about this man, and that brought some surprises. In the 1970s, carbon dating proved that this skeleton was no more than 10,000 years old, meaning that he lived in the Mesolithic period. More recent DNA testing revealed that Cheddar Man likely had the dark skin usually associated with sub-Saharan Africa. Previously, anthropologists had assumed that *Homo sapiens* developed lighter skin soon after leaving Africa and moving to Europe around 50,000 years ago (fair skin is more efficient at absorbing UV light and helps to avoid vitamin D deficiency in areas where there is less available sunlight). Cheddar Man suggested that this was not so, and subsequent DNA testing on other Mesolithic skeletons has confirmed that dark skin remained a feature in the early hunter-gatherers of Europe for far longer than anyone had suspected.

While no artifacts or tools were discovered with Cheddar Man, findings in other parts of Europe have provided clues that tell us that the cultural, religious, and artistic life of these early people was more sophisticated and diverse than was previously imagined.

Chapter Three

Stone Age Art and Religion

"Drawing is still basically the same as it has been since prehistoric times."

—Keith Haring

For a very long time, most guesses about the lifestyle of hunter-gatherers in Europe and elsewhere suggested that life was a constant struggle to find food and was generally cut short by famine, disease, or injury. However, a number of discoveries tell us that these people lived a more complex and vibrant life than was first believed.

Art seems to have been an important part of life for Mesolithic people. While cave paintings existed already in the Paleolithic era, it seems that this art form expanded into new forms and was carried out in new areas during the Mesolithic period. Some Mesolithic art was still carried out in caves, but due to the warmer climate, a great deal more was executed in open-air sites such as cliff faces and sheer rock faces, often chosen because these areas were protected from the elements by overhanging outcrops of rock. While Paleolithic paintings were generally representations of animals, Mesolithic paintings generally depict humans, either individuals or groups, often involved in activities such as hunting. A great deal of such paintings have been discovered on the northern coast of the Mediterranean Sea and particularly in southern Spain. This art is vivid, stylized, and well executed and, for the first time, depicts people involved in everyday tasks such as collecting food and, in one instance, apparently dancing.

What we don't know is just why Mesolithic people started producing this art on such a scale (and it seems likely that, as many paintings were in open-air sites, the majority have probably vanished over the last 10,000 years, so there was probably a great deal more than we now know of). One thing that has been noted about the paintings—particularly those discovered in southern Spain—is that they seem to be placed in what appear to us to be odd locations. Some have been painted in areas where, a short distance away, there seem to have been more suitable, more easily accessible, and more sheltered sites. This suggests that the sites themselves may have been chosen because they have particular significance.

It is possible, though of course we cannot be certain, that these paintings were linked to some cultural, magical, or religious significance. That may be linked with the fact that, from the late Paleolithic period, *Homo sapiens* began burying their dead in specific places. This was clearly more than just a way of disposing of bodies to avoid the spread of disease; many Mesolithic-era graves contain not just skeletons but also items such as tools and weapons—things that would have been very precious. A number of cemeteries have been discovered throughout Europe and elsewhere from this period, some containing over 50 sets of remains. One notable discovery is that some of these grave sites seem to have been in use for extended periods, in some cases for hundreds of years.

One of the largest Stone Age cemeteries discovered to date is the Zvejnieki burial ground located on the shores of Lake Burtnieks in northern Latvia. This site seems to have been used during the Mesolithic and early Neolithic eras and is thought to contain at least 400 burials of men, women, and children. Many were found to have been buried with distinctive animal tooth pendants, and some (both men and women) were buried with hunting and fishing equipment, including harpoons and spears. Clearly, not all members of social groups could have been buried in these sites or they would have contained far more remains. Were these high-status individuals or perhaps even proto-kings? Were they priests or shamans? Like so many aspects of Stone Age life, the answer is that we really don't know.

The fact that many remains were interred with tools, weapons, and other artifacts suggests an element of ritual. However, though it has been the subject of intense debate, no one is agreed that this signifies a belief in an afterlife and a disincarnate soul. It certainly seems that Mesolithic people believed that the dead might have a need for the things that they had used in life, but just what that signifies in terms of religious beliefs, we can only guess.

Other discoveries that also date from the Mesolithic era simply increase the mystery of just what it was that our ancestors believed in. One of the most baffling was a site that is now known as Gobekli Tepe, located near the city of Urfa in southeastern Turkey. The site was first discovered by a German archeologist, Klaus

Schmidt, in the 1990s. What he discovered changed our view of the Mesolithic world and introduced new mysteries that continue to baffle historians.

Schmidt discovered a number of circular stone enclosures, with the largest being over 65 feet (20 meters) in diameter. In the center of this enclosure were two very large stone columns, intricately carved with stylized images of human figures; this is (to date) the oldest known monumental structure ever created by humans. The columns are over 15 feet tall (5 meters) and must each weigh at least 10 tons. The truly startling discovery was that these columns and the enclosure in which they stand were erected around 9,600 BCE when the Mesolithic period had barely begun. Subsequently, more enclosures were added to the site, but whatever these were, they weren't homes or even palaces—no trace of habitation has been found in the complex of structures in Gobekli Tepe. Schmidt believed that the structure with the columns in it was a temple, and he may be right. But we have no idea of just what the people who might have worshipped in such a temple may have believed in, and we have no idea at all of how people who had only stone tools available to them could quarry, transport, and carve 10-ton stone columns.

New techniques and new technology mean that our knowledge of the Stone Age world is constantly expanding. But the more that we learn, the more we come to understand that we really don't know anything about the beliefs or inner life of these people.

Chapter Four

Agriculture and the Neolithic Era

"For a novelist, the great thing about the Stone Age people is that we know virtually nothing about their beliefs."

—Michelle Paver

Although the discovery of art and structures like those at Gobekli Tepe raise fascinating questions about Stone Age religion and culture, the most fundamental change to human society came from something seemingly more mundane: the development of agriculture. In fact, the beginning of the Neolithic era is generally accepted as the beginning of the first attempts by humans not just to gather and hunt available food but to grow crops that could be harvested. This is known as the Neolithic Revolution (or the First Agricultural Revolution).

Like so many aspects of the Stone Age, there wasn't a single point or location at which agriculture was suddenly employed. It seems to have developed relatively slowly and at different times in different areas. The change brought about by agriculture and the domestication of animals ended the nomadic lifestyle associated with hunter-gatherers who were forced to migrate to follow the animals they hunted. Agriculture meant that people could live for the first time in permanent settlements, and populations were able to grow as new technology produced more food.

Study of archeological findings suggests that the first plants to be cultivated in Europe were cereals, probably including barley, wheat, and rye. Later, other plants such as peas, lentils, chickpeas, and flax became common. In Asia, people began to domesticate millet and rice (traces of the first known rice paddies have been dated to 7,000 BCE in China). The spread of agriculture meant a fundamental change in the lifestyle of human cultures in this period. For the first time, it was possible to store surplus food.

Animals were also domesticated widely for the first time in this period. These included pigs (bred from wild boar), goats, sheep, and cattle. Animals provided not just meat and skins but also milk. For most of history before the beginning of the Neolithic era, the vast majority of *Homo sapiens* are believed to have been lactose-intolerant (unable to digest dairy products), but as the domestication of animals and the production of milk increased, many people were capable of producing lactase, the enzyme which breaks down lactose and is needed to digest dairy products.

The change to agricultural food production and the abandonment of a nomadic hunter-gatherer lifestyle also led directly to the creation of the first towns and even a few cities. Excavations in Catalhoyuk, a site in southern Turkey, have revealed a complex of permanent houses packed so closely together that residents could only enter their homes via holes in the roof! At its peak, it is believed that up to 8,000 people lived in this proto-city, which was occupied from around 7,500 BCE to 6,000 BCE. To date, Catalhoyuk is the oldest example of what we would now call an urban environment, and fascinatingly, studies have shown that it brought new hazards for the people who lived there.

Traces of animal and human feces have been found inside some of the houses, suggesting that sanitation wasn't something considered during its construction. Unsurprisingly, up to 30% of all the human remains recovered from the site show possible signs of bacterial infections. The teeth of adult remains were also in very poor condition—a result of eating a diet that was rich in whole grains that wore down the teeth.

Perhaps the most surprising finding of a study of the remains recovered from Catalhoyuk is proof of something that was, at the time, probably entirely new: urban violence. A number of the skulls recovered from this area indicate that the people involved were killed by a blow to the head from behind. A number of other skulls showed evidence of healed wounds seemingly caused by spherical projectiles, probably launched from a slingshot. No earlier Stone Age remains show similar signs of violence, and it has been claimed that this increased violence was a direct result of the stress and overcrowding that was part of the earliest towns and cities like Catalhoyuk.

Agriculture and the settled lifestyle it allowed permitted the human population to grow and to congregate in large, permanent settlements, but that brought its own hazards in the form of overcrowding, disease, and even intra-personal violence. However, a larger food supply also allowed individuals to focus for the first time on activities that were not directly related to gathering food. Among many other things, this led to the building of boats and the first voyages of exploration ever undertaken by *Homo sapiens*.

Chapter Five

Stone Age Exploration

*"In every island of the Aegean Sea, on almost
every barren rock I might say, are found
abundant traces of a vast prehistoric empire."*

—James Theodore Bent

Hominids seem to have been sailing the oceans
for a very long time indeed. Archeological
excavation on the island of Luzon in the
Philippines found the skeleton of a rhinoceros
that appeared to have been butchered, as well as
a large number of stone tools. However, the
skeleton was dated to around 600,000 years ago,
long before *Homo sapiens* began their expansion
out of Africa. Whoever left these marks could
only have traveled to Luzon by sea.

Stone Age people began to build simple
boats from a very early period. This was a simple
necessity for those who lived close to large rivers
or the sea, as it allowed not just easy transport
but also more productive fishing. The earliest

boats were probably no more than single logs or a few pieces of timber lashed together to form a simple raft. However, during the later Paleolithic era, more sophisticated vessels were developed in various parts of the world.

The earliest human settlers in Australia, for example, arrived there around 50,000 years ago, according to archeological excavations. These people could only have reached Australia by boat, and this would have involved a voyage that would have been out of sight of land, a perilous undertaking for a Stone Age sailor. It seems very likely that these people came from the Sundaland Peninsula in Asia and sailed on bamboo rafts, possibly with simple sails. All over the Stone Age world, people began building larger and more effective vessels and using them to explore new lands.

Canoes, formed by hollowing out tree trunks with stone tools, have been recovered that date from the Mesolithic period. It has also been surmised that Mesolithic and Neolithic seafarers may have used boats made from wood and animal skin (coracle), though no archeological evidence has been found to support this to date. These small boats would most likely have been used for fishing, but they could also have been used for longer journeys of exploration. We know that Mesolithic and Neolithic people did explore by sea because they were able to colonize islands that cannot be reached in any other way (for example, Shetland and the Outer Hebrides off the coast of Scotland and Crete and other islands in the Mediterranean).

Few larger boats from the Stone Age have been found, but one discovery in Kuwait in 2002 hints at what might have been possible. Archeologists working at a site in Sabiyah, a site now deep in the desert of Kuwait, found the remains of what appears to be a boat made of reeds fixed with bitumen. The area in which this was discovered would have been on the shores of the Persian Gulf in 5,500 BCE, the period to which the artifacts have been dated. This seems to have been a seagoing vessel, though what it would have been used for is not known. Could this have been a merchant vessel plying early trade routes in the region? We can't know for certain, but it certainly implies that Stone Age people were capable of constructing ships for long seagoing journeys.

Excavations at the Kaylu rock shelter, a cave-like burial site on the shores of the Caspian Sea, revealed ornamental beads made from the shells of a particular species of cockle. However, that cockle and beads made from it weren't from the area around Kaylu but from other cultures on the Caspian, strongly suggesting the Stone Age seafarers sailed and perhaps traded on this sea.

The question of just what type of ships Stone Age seafarers might have used and precisely where they sailed and why are still matters of debate. We know that these people did take to the ocean because of the spread of *Homo sapiens* to islands, but we know very little about the vessels they used or the reasons for these perilous voyages.

Chapter Six

Stone Age Work and Trade

"We wear the cape of civilization but our souls live in the Stone Age."

—Nizar Qabbani

For a very long time, historians and anthropologists assumed that the life of Stone Age people was short and that it involved an incessant quest for food and a constant battle against the prospect of starvation. More recently, this view has been revised. There is a growing belief that the people of the Stone Age may actually have had more leisure time than most people do today and may have enjoyed a lifestyle very different from the constant struggle originally envisaged.

During the late Paleolithic and Mesolithic periods, the vast majority of *Homo sapiens* lived in relatively small groups of hunter-gatherers.

Inevitably, even a fairly small group of people will quickly deplete the food resources in the immediate area. The only solutions are to hunt and forage further afield or to migrate to a new base. The latter seems to have been the most common solution adopted by Stone Age people. They migrated to new settlements throughout the year to keep themselves close to sources of food. That, of course, has important side effects. Housing must of necessity be temporary, and any goods must be easily transportable. There is simply no point in having possessions if they become a burden each time the group relocates.

But while these people may have had few possessions, their lives may have been very different from what was previously imagined. In the 1970s, studies were carried out to examine the few remaining hunter-gatherer societies. These included groups of aboriginal people in Australia and Africa, and the results were surprising. In areas where game and other food were plentiful (as we assume they were in the Mesolithic and Neolithic forests), people spent, on average, less than four hours each day acquiring food. One extended study of hunter-gatherer groups in Africa found that the average over a one-year period was actually less than two hours per day.

Of course, this acquisition of food is not continuous. There are periods when hunters spend days or even weeks engaged in the hunt before they return to camp. But at that point, they have provided sufficient food, and hunting temporarily stops. One study produced in the 1970s—*Stone Age economics* by Marshall Sahlins—concluded that for Stone Age hunter-gatherers, "the food quest is intermittent, leisure abundant, and there is a greater amount of sleep in the daytime per capita per year than in any other condition of society." That's interesting and quite different from the image of grinding hardship that most previous studies had assumed.

We also know that trade in the Stone Age seems to have been widespread. We know this simply because archeological findings have uncovered artifacts in certain areas that have either been brought in complete from other areas or were made from raw materials only available in another part of the world. That too suggests a much more complex and interconnected culture than might have been expected. It also poses a question: just how did Stone Age people trade given that they had nothing that was the equivalent of money? The notion of having tokens that denoted value did not begin until the

Bronze Age when the first metal coins were produced, so just how did Stone Age trade work?

Most evidence suggests that there was relatively little trade during the Paleolithic era. It seems likely that hunter-gatherer groups collected only what they could have used immediately, leaving no surplus to trade and, in any case, no means of storing or transporting any surplus. As farming became more common during the late Mesolithic and Neolithic eras, food surpluses began to become available for the first time, and new and more sophisticated tools became objects that could be traded. It seems very likely that, as food surpluses became available for the first time, this freed members of communities to specialize in the production of things such as pottery, jewelry, and weapons, which seem to have become the focus of trade.

We know virtually nothing about Stone Age trade networks beyond the obvious fact that they must have existed in order to account for the discovery of non-indigenous artifacts in Stone Age archeological sites. There is no evidence that Stone Age people had any equivalent of the notion of money that emerged later during the Bronze Age, so the assumption is that there must have been some system of inter-tribal relationships that enabled them to barter one kind of item for another, or perhaps for food. We have no idea how such people established relative value, an essential element of trade; how many flint arrowheads equaled the value of a pendant made from sea shells? Yet somehow, these people overcame this problem and were able to trade with one another.

What we are coming to understand is that Stone Age culture and society were very different from what we might have previously imagined. And that seems to be confirmed by some of the most notable projects undertaken by these people: the building of monumental structures that we still do not fully understand.

Chapter Seven

Stone Age Technology and Architecture

"Stone Age. Bronze Age. Iron Age. We define entire epics of humanity by the technology they use."

—Reed Hastings

Perhaps no Stone Age structure has caused more debate nor potentially offered a greater insight into Stone Age culture and society than Stonehenge on Salisbury Plain in England. We simply don't know what the purpose of this vast structure was, nor, most importantly, how it was built.

Work on this site began somewhere around 3,000 BCE, and the great stones at its center were erected around 2,500 BCE, at the end of the Neolithic period and before metalworking became common in Britain. Archeological excavations across Britain suggest that, during that period, there were few towns where the population would have gathered and few even very small collections of houses. Almost all Stone Age buildings that have been found from this period in Britain are single buildings or small farmsteads. That's significant because the completion of Stonehenge would have required the presence of a large workforce for an extended period. Just where did these people come from, and how were they gathered together?

Stonehenge consists of three separate but linked elements: a large circular ditch (probably the first element to be completed), a system of standing bluestones, and an outer ring of huge sarsen stones. We know that these are not from the immediate area of Stonehenge. The bluestones (each weighing around 4 tons) originate in the Preseli Hills of Wales, almost 200 miles (320 kilometers) from Stonehenge. The massive sarsens were quarried around 20 miles (32 kilometers) away on the Marlborough Downs, but each weighs over 20 tons! Just how did Stone Age people quarry these huge stones and then move them over considerable distances?

The most generally accepted theory is that the sarsens were moved on rollers from the area where they were cut to shape (using only flint and stone tools) before being moved over the rolling countryside to the spot where they were erected. It has been estimated that it would have taken at least 100 people to move a single sarsen, and originally, there were over 80 of these massive stones at Stonehenge (though only 52 remain today). No one is entirely certain how long it would have taken to bring all the sarsens to the site, but this must certainly have been a major commitment in terms of a workforce that would have been needed probably for tens of years.

Moving the bluestones from the mountains of Wales, although they weren't quite as large, must have been an even greater challenge. They were probably transported at least part of the way by sea, but large parts of their long journey would have required the same laborious process of rolling them on logs.

Then there is the problem of lifting them into place. Just how did Stone Age people lift sarsen stones weighing more than 20 tons over 20 feet (6 meters) into the air to place them on top of the standing stones? There are a number of theories, but to date, no one has been able to find any evidence of how it was done.

We know that the quarrying, transport, and erection of these giant stones must have represented a mammoth undertaking to a culture that generally existed only as a series of isolated farms and small hamlets. The bigger question is: why did Stone Age people invest so much time and energy over such an extended period to build this structure? Stonehenge certainly seems to have been a place with ceremonial importance—a broad avenue has been found leading toward the site, and the outer ditch and earth wall would originally have been more than six feet (two meters) tall, concealing what was happening inside.

It's very easy to imagine processions approaching the site via the avenue and then performing some form of ritual inside, but we have no idea what deities the priests or shamans involved might have worshipped nor what the purpose of such a ceremony might have been. Evidence of a complex of Stone Age buildings nearby, at Durrington Walls, suggests that there might once have been a complex of buildings that may have been associated with this site. This doesn't seem to have been a town, and its purpose is unknown, though these may have been ceremonial buildings associated with the main structure.

We know that Stonehenge was used as a burial site; more than 60 graves have been found close by, but we don't know if this was the reason it was created or whether these graves were later placed in proximity to an existing sacred site. It's also known that the stones that form Stonehenge were erected with astrological significance. Both sarsens and bluestones align precisely with sunrise at the summer solstice and sunset at the winter solstice (respectively the longest and shortest days of the year). The stones that actually frame the rising and setting sun at these times are the most carefully worked of all, being shaped to frame the sun as it appears and disappears. The avenue that leads to Stonehenge is also precisely aligned with the point at which the sun rises on the summer solstice. These things are so precise that they cannot be coincidence. Whoever designed Stonehenge was aware of and able to predict the movement of the sun with extreme accuracy. That's not the kind of knowledge that we usually associate with the people of the Stone Age, yet this massive monument proves it beyond doubt.

All the evidence tells us that during the time when Stonehenge was created, the population of England lived in scattered farms and a handful of tiny hamlets. There were no towns and certainly no cities, but there must have been some form of overarching social organization that allowed a workforce of hundreds or perhaps thousands to be gathered, controlled, fed, housed, and retained for extended periods. These people were then able to quarry, transport, and erect stones of massive size and to place them in positions that reflect astronomical knowledge that could only have come from many years of careful observation and recording. Perhaps more than any other artifact from the Stone Age, Stonehenge tells us that the knowledge, culture, and social structure that must have been needed to build it were far more complex and sophisticated than our current estimate of what Stone Age life may have looked like.

By 1,500 BCE, knowledge of the purpose for which Stonehenge had been erected seems to have vanished. The culture that built it and the techniques and tools they used were as mysterious to their Bronze Age successors as they are now.

Chapter Eight

Stone Age Medicine and Health

"Deep down, most of us find ourselves still in the Stone Age of superstition."

—Helen Hayes

Life expectancy in the Stone Age is difficult to cite with any degree of accuracy. When historians first began to describe this period, they assumed that most people did not live long beyond the age of 20, but today, that view has been challenged. Most Stone Age remains that have been discovered are indeed of people aged between 20 and 40, and most statistical surveys suggest an average age for Stone Age people of around 30 to 35 years. However, that doesn't mean that most Stone Age people died before the age of 40, as any average for the period is biased by high rates of infant mortality. Recent studies looked at surviving groups of hunter-gatherer people and discovered that, if infant mortality is removed, the median age of death is between 70 and 80 years, about the same as for modern, developed societies.

In the modern world, we have medicine and healthcare that help prevent deaths from injury and illness, but we are also contending with growing levels of obesity and diseases such as cancer that seem to have been virtually unknown to Stone Age people. It is entirely possible that average life expectancy is not much better now than it was in the Stone Age; it's just that the main causes of premature death have changed.

Stone Age remains do show the presence of a range of conditions that might have shortened life, such as osteoarthritis (a degenerative joint condition caused by repetitive strain), rickets (a condition caused by poor diet that can lead to soft bones in children), as well as bone deformity and bone wastage, attributable to a diet that lacks vitamin D. Many Stone Age women (and their children) seem to have died during childbirth, and it is assumed that things like relatively minor injuries might have led to infections that would have been incapacitating or even fatal.

There is a general assumption (mainly based on observation of surviving groups of hunter-gatherers) that Stone Age people would have had some knowledge of the medicinal use of plants and herbs, though no evidence to prove this has been found to date. However, there is evidence that Stone Age people had far more effective medical care than we might once have thought. For example, in 2022, a Stone Age body was recovered from the Liang Tebo cave in Borneo. These were found to be the remains of a young man or woman, probably aged around 20. Carbon dating showed that this person had lived at least 30,000 years ago. What was surprising was that this person had a leg amputated several years before death. Examination by medical experts showed that the amputation had been carried out with "considerable surgical skill," and the patient had obviously survived, something that implies an ability to control blood loss and prevent post-surgery infection. That appears to demonstrate considerable medical knowledge and skill, things that are generally not thought to have existed until the Bronze Age and later.

Other Stone Age remains have also provided evidence of patients who survived complex surgery. Remains from the Paleolithic and Neolithic periods have provided skulls that have been trepanned—a medical procedure that involves creating a large hole in the skull. Many show signs of subsequent bone growth, proving that these people survived a very challenging operation. Flint blades were extremely sharp (some people claim that they were actually shaper than modern scalpels!), so Stone Age people certainly had the equipment to perform surgery. Still, the fact that patients survived afterward indicates more detailed knowledge than what was previously suspected.

Just like the vast structures of Stonehenge, this evidence of survival after major surgery tells us that Stone Age people had, in some respects, more knowledge than those who came after.

Chapter Nine

Everyday Life in the Stone Age

"The Stone Age gave us arrowheads and eventually knives, and that allowed us to kill animals in ways you couldn't before."

—Neal Barnard

What we know of daily life in the Stone Age comes from archeological findings, and given that these only include things that have survived for thousands of years, they only give fragmentary glimpses of what life may have been like.

In the Paleolithic era, people lived in small family groups in simple, temporary homes made from wood and perhaps covered in animal skin (they may have been similar to the tepees used by the native people of North America). They used fire for cooking and to provide warmth. In areas where there were naturally occurring caves, people may also have used these as homes, refuges, and places to gather. That is why Stone Age people were originally called cavemen, though it seems likely that only a lucky few had such homes, and these were probably only used during certain periods of the years as most early humans were nomadic.

Their food came from the animals they hunted—mainly deer, auroch, and bison (in some places, also woolly mammoth)—using simple bone and flint spears and axes. They cooked the meat from these animals over fires and supplemented their diet with berries, nuts, and, if they were close to the sea, fish and shellfish. A few seem to have taken time out from the daily search for food to gather minerals, burnt bone meal, and charcoal, which they mixed with water, blood, and tree saps to create pigments that they used to make paintings in the caves in which they lived and on rock faces and cliffs.

In the Mesolithic era, the warming climate and receding ice sheets allowed these people to expand into new areas. By that time, *Homo sapiens* was the only remaining human species, and these people began to build larger (though still temporary) homes, with wooden structures over an excavated base, centered on a hearth for cooking and warmth. Their stone-working skills improved, and they were able to produce more refined arrows and harpoons. For the most part, people retained a nomadic, hunter-gatherer lifestyle that wasn't much changed from the previous era, but gradually, imperceptibly, new ideas on agriculture began to emerge.

The Neolithic era saw a fundamental change to the way in which Stone Age people lived. They began to farm and domesticate animals for the first time, and they began to live in larger and more permanent settlements. New agricultural implements such as plows were introduced for the first time, though of course these were still made from stone and wood. In locations such as Catalhoyuk in Turkey, people began the first construction of cities, and these saw people living for the first time close together in permanent dwellings.

The change to a fixed, agricultural lifestyle brought food surpluses that meant that not all members of the group were required to be directly involved in production, and that led to an expansion of specialists who produced pottery and improved tools. But this change also introduced these people to the drawbacks of urban living—overcrowding, intra-personal violence, and the rapid spread of infectious diseases. By the end of the Neolithic period, human society had evolved to a form much closer to that we see today, with all the benefits and disbenefits that was to bring.

This, as far as we are aware, was the basic outline of life during the Stone Age, but there are some notable gaps. We don't know anything at all about the social structures of Stone Age communities or, for example, anything about the role of women. Studies suggest that the average life expectancy for Stone Age women was much lower than for men, probably accounted for by deaths in childbirth. From the way in which some high-status individuals were buried, Stone Age people seem to have had beliefs about what happened after death, and by inference, some form of religion, but we have no idea what form this took or how important a part it played in everyday life. A few individuals seemed to have knowledge of things like how to perform surgery, but we don't know where this knowledge came from or how significant medicine and those who practiced it were to Stone Age people.

And finally, we have no knowledge of large-scale social structures during any period of the Stone Age. But the construction of sites such as Gobekli Tepe in Turkey and Stonehenge in England—both of which would have required the gathering, direction, and care of thousands of workers—tells us that there must have been, at least in some places and at certain times, such capability for large-scale organization and direction.

So, when we look at the everyday life in the Stone Age, while there are certain things that we can deduce through the artifacts and remains that have been discovered, there is clearly a great deal more to be learned about this fascinating period.

Chapter Ten

The End of the Stone Age

"The Stone Age may return on the gleaming wings of Science."

—Winston Churchill

Just like its beginning, the end of the Stone Age didn't happen at one time. It was a gradual process that emerged at different times and in different places, with new knowledge that spread and other knowledge that was ignored or simply forgotten. For this reason, there is considerable overlap between the end of the Neolithic era and the beginning of the next major technological development: the Bronze Age. Some historians refer to this period of overlap as the Chalcolithic (Copper-Stone) Age to indicate that the end of using stone tools and the beginning of metalworking spanned an extended period of time and happened in parallel.

The Stone Age seems to have ended first in an area known as Mesopotamia, a fertile plain between the Tigris and Euphrates Rivers in present-day Iraq and Kuwait. The Sumerians, a people whose origins are still mysterious, arrived in this area and brought with them new knowledge and new technologies. These included sophisticated farming approaches, including the use of complex irrigation systems to improve the production from farms.

Around 3,500 BCE, people in Mesopotamia began to work metal for the first time. This principally involved copper, though even this wasn't entirely new—the earliest copper artifacts have been discovered in Anatolia in present-day Turkey dating all the way back to 7,500 BCE. What the people in Mesopotamia did differently was that they employed new casting techniques that allowed them to reliably produce metal tools and weapons that were superior to their equivalents made from stone.

These improved tools and weapons made agriculture more efficient. For example, new metal axes made it much easier to clear land for agriculture, and the use of metal plows and hoe-like implements made the land more productive. These things made it possible for a relatively small workforce to produce enough food to feed everyone. This led to the rapid development of urban centers housing thousands of people and the emergence of a more stratified and specialized society where artisans and traders produced and exchanged the new metal artifacts, and rulers, effectively the first kings, presided over large populations housed in a relatively small area. This specialization also led directly to major developments such as the first emergence of writing and the first systematic approaches to science and astronomy.

Knowledge of the new technology spread rapidly. The first metal artifacts from the Harappan Civilization in the Indus River Valley in present-day India have been dated to around 3,300 BCE. By around 3,100 BCE, metalworking had spread to Egypt, and around 100 years later, metalworking had become common in the Aegean in the area formed by present-day Greece. From these regions, this knowledge gradually spread to other parts of Europe, though it took some time to reach the most distant areas. In Britain, for example, metalworking did not seem to become common until perhaps as late as 2,100 BCE.

It is difficult to overestimate the importance of the arrival of metalworking to human civilization. Simple things that we now take for granted, like nails, became available for the first time and revolutionized building and ship construction. Metal tools allowed much easier working of stone, and the kilns that were used to produce metal also led to the development of brick-making. Suddenly, it was possible to build larger, multi-story structures. These led directly to the building of the first large cities.

Of course, metalworking also led to the creation of new and more effective weapons and to the development of personal armor. Cultures that embraced these new technologies quickly found themselves with a notable advantage over those that did not, and mighty empires, including the Akkadian and Assyrian, grew rapidly from the military advantage that the adoption of metalworking provided them. Excavations from this period have identified the sites of what appear to be the first-ever large-scale battles involving large armies armed with metal weapons.

For example, archeological digs in the Tollense River Valley in northern Germany revealed what appears to have been the site of a very large battle. The remains of over 140 individuals were located at this site (many showing signs of grievous injury), and experts have claimed that this may have been the site of a battle that might have involved up to 4,000 warriors, which would have made it one of the largest battles of this period. We don't know just who was involved in fighting this battle, but what is notable is that artifacts recovered include a mix of stone and flint weapons and more advanced and effective metal versions. Could this have been a battle between the remnants of a Stone Age people and another group using metal weapons? If so, it seems unlikely that the side using Stone Age technology would have been victorious.

This battle site provides us with a useful analogy for the impact of the arrival of the Bronze Age. Metal tools, farming implements, weapons, and armor are simply much more effective and durable than their Stone Age equivalents. The Stone Age period died out for the simple reason that cultures that maintained this old technology could not compete, in terms of agricultural production or on the battlefield, with those that adopted the new technology. The adoption of metalworking wasn't just a new phase in human evolution; it was a revolution that, in a remarkably short space of time, saw ways of life that had been maintained for hundreds of thousands of years replaced with entirely new approaches. New urban centers emerged, and they brought with them advances such as writing, science, and technology.

The end of the Stone Age brought with it the beginning of an entirely new way of life for people around the world, and one that still has echoes in today's lifestyle where the majority of people live in urban centers and pursue employment that is not directly related to the production of food.

Conclusion

The Stone Age covers over 99% of all human history, but it is a period about which we still know relatively little. It was also a period that saw the gradual acceleration of change. The Paleolithic era lasted for millions of years, during which the human species seem to have made relatively few advances and where the human lifestyle changed little. For us, perhaps the most important development during this era was that *Homo sapiens* became the dominant human species while all others disappeared. We are not at all certain why or how this happened. It doesn't seem to have been the result of conquest; archeological evidence suggests that *Homo sapiens* and other human species had co-existed for hundreds of thousands of years. But by the beginning of the Mesolithic era, only *Homo sapiens* remained, and that species colonized every part of our planet.

It has been suggested that this was because our species had more effective cognitive abilities and was simply better at devising strategies for survival, but this isn't at all certain. Neanderthals, for example, made tools, buried their dead, and may have produced art, which suggests a similar ability for reasoning, but Neanderthals vanished while our species remained and spread. This spread became more pronounced during the Mesolithic era, which also saw the end of the Last Ice Age and a global change in climate that saw ice sheets receding and vast new areas becoming available for habitation.

Defining dates for the Stone Age is problematic and something that is still debated. Generally, it is accepted that the Mesolithic era began around 10,000 years ago and lasted around 5,000 years, a much shorter span than the preceding Paleolithic era. During the Mesolithic era, people were still operating as small family groups of nomadic hunter-gatherers, but there were clearly inter-tribal connections that led to the spread of new knowledge. This can be seen in evidence of trade and the sharing of more advanced technologies that allowed the creation of more useful stone tools.

The Neolithic era was shorter still, only around half as long as the Mesolithic at 2,000 years, but this era saw the beginning of changes that would transform human life and culture. Most notable was the beginning of agriculture and the creation of the first permanent settlements. These were still small compared to what would follow, but they were the first time in human history that not everyone had to be involved in the acquisition of food. That in turn led to the emergence of artisans who specialized in the production of certain items and most likely also to the emergence of priests or shamans (who we may regard as the first proto-scientists) who were probably the first humans to have the time to think about the planet on which we live and its relationship to the cosmos.

One of the most notable things about the Stone Age is how little we still know about it. Some of the mysteries are huge. How were Stone Age doctors able to perform successful surgery? How was it possible to draw together the huge workforces needed to create structures like Stonehenge and Gobekli Tepe? Others are less obvious but no less intriguing. What were the social structures of Stone Age people? Did they believe in the afterlife and have religion? Why did they create art?

The study of the Stone Age continues, and every new discovery expands our knowledge a little. When the term Stone Age was first used in the nineteenth century, there was a general assumption that the people of those times were brutish and backward. Subsequent discoveries have changed that view, and some people now regard the Stone Age as a period when humans lived in harmony with the natural environment and probably had very different values from those who followed. The only thing we can be certain of is that there will be future discoveries that will expand our knowledge further and that, one day perhaps, we will gain a clearer understanding of the Stone Age origins of human culture and society.

Bibliography

Clottes, J., Lewis-Williams, D. (1998). *The Shamans of Prehistory*.

Harari, Y. (2018). *Sapiens; A Brief History of Humankind*.

Sahlins, M. (1972). *Stone Age Economics*.

Spindler, K. (1995). *The Man in the Ice: The Discovery of a 5,000-Year-Old Body Reveals the Secrets of the Stone Age*.

"Stone Age Humans Conducted Surgical Amputation 31,000 Years Ago". September 2022. *Sci News*.

"700,000-Year-Old Butchered Rhino Pushes Back Ancient Human Arrival in the Philippines". May 2018. *Smithsonian Magazine*.

"First modern Britons had 'dark to black' skin, Cheddar Man DNA analysis reveals". February 2018. *The Guardian*.

"Early Seafarers May Have Traveled the Caspian Sea". June 2023. Archaeological Institute of America.

Made in United States
Cleveland, OH
10 January 2025